This book is dedicated to
Miel de Botton
A beautiful agate
brought my patron
into being.

A note from the author

Special thanks to:

James Wallace who continues to make my handsome, hand-crafted limited edition elephant poo books. He is my inspiration as a poet and an artist.

The goddesses Gilly, Gabes, Gina & Sam at "Buddha On A Bicycle", 27 Endell Street, Covent Garden, WC2H 9BA. The first shop to sell my book in London and the best crystals and gifts in town.

Sîan Dobson for introducing me to her beloved David Burrows who is the illustrator-genius-mad fella who designed the front and back of the book! I thank you.

Ira Silverberg, Sterling Lord Literistic (New York), for shaking my hand and making me feel a million dollars at Curtis Brown.

Vegetarian establishments in London: "The Gate", "Food For Thought" (especially Steve Wilcox), "World Food Café" and "Mildreds". "David Bann" - Edinburgh. Nadine Abensur, author of "The Cranks Bible".

William Burdett Coutts, Assembly Rooms at "The Edinburgh Festival 2009" for putting on my poetry show. Steve Morrison, All3Media for his kind heart + Annika Magnberg for her sensational singing in the show.

Brian Patten, poet, for all his glorious feedback.

Angele July for her natty PR.

The Ditti 8, especially Marnie Moyle for her poetry swing (Greenoak Furniture). www.greenoakfurniture.co.uk.

Biggest thanks of all to my adorable Martin Seager for creating the song "Wear A Mask" whilst walking our dogs Billy, Valentine, Wilf and George (not forgetting our lovely cats Ragz and Dolly).

First published by UCV book in 2009.

This edition published 2011 by The Word Café.

www.thewordcafe.biz

The right of Julie Mullen to be identified as author of this work "Erotic Poetry For Vegans & Vegetarians" has been asserted by her in accordance with the Copyright, Designs and Patents Act 1988.

Front and back covers designed by David Burrows©.

Erotic Poetry For Vegans & Vegetarians is
printed on recycled paper made from elephant dung and other materials

Printed and bound in Great Britain by Barnwell Print Ltd. Aylsham, Norfolk NR11 6SU

British Library Cataloguing in Publication Data; a catalogue record for this book is available from The British Library

ISBN 9780956356536

Contents

THE WELL-HUNG MUNG BEAN   1

TO A QUEER KUMQUAT   2

BEYOND THE CARROT   4

PINK FIR APPLE   10

MY MANE IS KEN   12

SHE-SHE   15

HALLOUMI   18

ON A SWALLOW'S ARM   23

A MUSING ON RED   25

EROTICHIM V EROTICHER   29

MARROW ME   32

THE LANDSCAPE MAN   36

ANGELICA & HER BRAZILIAN   42

SEXY PIZZA   45

BENT NOT JUST CROOKED   46

TO BE VEGAN   48

Erotic Poetry
for Vegans
& Vegetarians

The Well-Hung Mung Bean

WHERE YOU BEEN Mung
  You're so well-hung Mung
Your song been sung Mung
Don't forgive and forget Mung
They use too much dung Mung

Well mung bean
I'm always looking out for the unseen
But you're a sight for sore eyes Mung
A truly *testoristic* flight Mung
A lady of the night Mung

JULIE MULLEN

To A Queer Kumquat

OH MASCARPONE
My Kumquat
Doth cream
Gingerly in your presence
'Twas a sticky date with those pecan petals
It turned me
A greengage fool for you my love!
Your Crème Anglaise
Doth make even a coconut pound cake rise!
You poach apricots
Then daily with a fistful of pistachios
Come clean
Don't just Crème Anglaise me
Crème Fraîche me!
Almond tart me
And my passion fruit
Will surely plum jam
Trifle and prune is me
You will crystallise

Then caramelise
And sear me with
Your quince apace
Henceforth love bring rosewater
To my fig quarter
Oh me Kumquat
Me
Oh me
Mascarpone
Me
Oh me
Crème Fraîche
Me
Oh oh me
Queen Baklava
Drizzle my roasted plums
And my mango is yours

JULIE MULLEN

Beyond the Carrot

HARRY WAS A veggie
Harry was my nice neighbour in his
elasticated cardigan
Tattyhatted
Fatted cravatted
He was a theatrical agent
Drinking red wine
And slinging the bottles into his very hip
Ecologically Sound
Black bin
He had dressed the bin in spankingly blue
underpants
Underpants for boxes?
Like they were cold standing out there

He had style but somehow
Just too old-fashioned for old-fashioned me
I kept away
I didn't like vegetarians

Then one day just after a
Battle of a day that made me weep on the train
I slipped past his ecologically sound black bin
    and neat undies
And I saw him naked
Coming out of the bath
He was standing there in the moonlight this
    November eve
All damp and vegetarian
And in the background I smelt carrots on the
    cook
So I slammed my door
Slammed it
For the hell of it
And for his carrots
And his tattyhattedness
And my loneliness
And my longing for
What lay beyond
The carrot

I went in and changed
I changed
And I changed again
Then I bathed and I threw in cabbages
And broccoli
And aubergine and
I bathed in these vegetables
Caressed them
Loved them
Joined them
The water was hot and steamy
I felt the earth
I felt the soil
I felt Harry's hat
I felt

I felt crazy but loved it
I felt awkward but shunned it
I felt
I was feeling for the first time

The bath water was raging now
And I
Underneath
These vegetables
Stewed
In
My
Own
Juices
Tumbling down
With Harry's nakedness
He was meat
I wanted meat
The meat of a man

I got out of the bath and I dripped wet
I got out of the bath and I dripped wet
Over to number 8
To Harry
He opened the door
He was still naked

I'd heard he bathed in vegetables
Lovingly bathed with them
Then cooked them
But I hadn't believed it
Until today when I smelt the carrot
Not boiling on his stove
But cooking in his bath

I went to his bed
I went to Harry's bed
And there I saw a head of cauliflower that
Made me feel like an elasticity of coming
An age
A time
A right time
We caressed the head together
Then a cabbage
And before I knew it
Harry had plunged me into Vegetarian Heaven
Vegetarian Heaven

Erotic Poetry for Vegans & Vegetarians

Why had I waited so long
To go veggie

JULIE MULLEN

Pink Fir Apple

HIS PINK FIR apple
Mashed
Boiled
Thrashed
Soiled
His pink fir apple

His pink fir apple
Dapple
Dimple
Sample
Luscious
His pink fir apple

His pink fir apple
Sieved
Buttery
Tip-top
Fat chip glory

His pink fir apple

His pink fir apple
Next to my pink
Next to me pink
Roll it around me
His pink fir apple

His pink fir apple
I want to stroke it
I want to soak it
I want to lick mayonnaise off it
To fry it
To bake it
To love it
His pink fir apple

JULIE MULLEN

My Mane is Ken

Asthanga Hatha Kundalini
Yogas that I do
My Sanskrit dreaming
Drew me
Draw me
Dreamily to you

I was
Donkey
Cat
+
Dog
Position B
Four eleven
Yards before my shoulder touched your toes
We went to
Heaven

My Hatha Kundalini

Yogic erotic vegan poses
Drew tiger lily darlings all comin'
Sweetly through their noses

My lion tongue
Your Sanskrit sighs
Those vegetarian celestial thighs
Your openness
To my vegan . . . pies . . .
Vegan pork pies

Your buttock formed
Alliance with my
Sanskrit earthly mane
My female erotic darlings
All link with
St. Germaine

I am Ken
Akin to kings
I do all manner of erotic things

I am yogic stew
Especially and emphatically for
You

Tonight when we are nestlin' on my futon
Here in Clapham
We'll roll out our mats
And see them gently overlappin'

I will announce my name
Is St. Germaine
Ok it's Ken it's Ken . . .
Oh Lara are you leavin' then?

She-She

S HE WAS LATE
She was waiting
She was coming
She was humming
She was in a taxi
She was getting waxy
She had no luggage
She had gently prepared
She was assuming
She was peeling
She was arriving
She was inviting
She was drawing her in
She was walking by
She was licking her lips
She was anticipating pips
She was revealing then peeling
She was sucking and squealing
She was in her elemental

She was feeling
She was receiving
She was neatly entwined
She was grossly red wined
She was lost in cucumber
She was touching her ink
She was giving a wink
She was rocking and rolling
She was uncontrolling
She was wet and all ripe
She was smoking her pipe
She was grimacing and sweating
She was with fruit
She was without
She was engaging and slim
She was altogether thin
She was alto
She was mezzo
She was soprano
She was piano
She was ready now

She was ripened now
She was wettened now
She was threatened now
She was injecting now
She was rejecting now
She was slicing now
She was juicing now
She was producing orange now
She was introducing blackberries now
She was inside now
She was an outsider now
She was slipping in
She was slipping out
She was proud and honest
She was slightly
She was there
She was her
She was long and luscious
She was with tall brushes
She was painting it on
She was Sent using BlackBerry from Orange

JULIE MULLEN

Halloumi

HE TOUCHED MY thigh tonight
The bus conductor
I only asked for a ticket to Archway
And before I knew it
A hairy arm came out of his cabin
Well at least I think it was an arm
It slightly tickled me and then it seemed to stop
    quite frozen
It stiffened up
I think . . .
I think it was an arm

I looked down eventually
After I enjoyed it for a bit
Because we were alone on the bus
At the depot
I was the only passenger on this
Bus
I looked down

And
There it was full blown
Not an arm at all
But a frozen chicken

The bus conductor laughed and said he had been
    given it
The chicken
As a gift from someone who worked in Iceland
He was a vegetarian, so would I like it?
Would I like it?
He was a vegetarian
And would I like it
Bloody cheek
I am a bloody vegetarian
I said
Frustrated
I walked away leaving him
With his frozen
Chicken

I sat down and
I began to thaw myself
I closed my eyes
Closed them
Closed them
Because he was handsome
Indian or Pakistani
a filmstarrilybeautifulhandsomeOHmyGOD sort of
    a man
Driving a bus with a rampant chicken
And I began to imagine what it would have been
    like
If his frozen fruity zip soldier
Yes his . . . his . . . ZIP soldier had
Come out of his little fridge
To check out my thigh
What then I thought
What then

My mind wandered to vegetarianism
And I couldn't get the thought of a

Erotic Poetry for Vegans & Vegetarians

Halloumi sandwich out of my head
I don't know why
Then and just then
I felt a warm feeling on my leg
I felt it creep up my thigh
Should I open my eyes?
Open my eyes
Open my eyes
No, enjoy it you veggie beast I thought
So I kept them shut
Tight shut
But kept my mouth moist
And inviting
Then I felt it on my lips
Gently
Very gently
I opened my eyes
And there in front of me
Right on cue
Was the chicken
The frozen chicken

Had made its way from the cabin
Defrosting
Denuded
Deluded
Delinquent
Begging me to respect it

Together we snuggled up
My halloumi sandwich a thing of the past

On A Swallow's Arm

A MAN ASKED me to suck on a lemon
I was innocent
Just strumming my follicle as you do
When you're waiting for life
To dream up some more bloody tragedy
A man
Plump
Like a lemon
Disturbed my insolence
In silence
I twisted and twiddled my hair
And disrupted a clear thunder thought
Bake off
I erupted
Bake off and get scooted
(I meant suited)
The lemon man curdled before me
His face like a melted tangerine

JULIE MULLEN

On a swallow's arm I walked away
Completing this dalliance

A Musing On Red

S OFT SOFT RED Red
Red Red soft soft
Bed Red ribbon

My honeysuckle pink sang
Scenting you to me
Sending me
To You

You, reeking of lost winters
Open windows
And messed up
Egyptian white
Sheets
Covered in our violets
Robin Red

Dead robin
Torn wings

JULIE MULLEN

Lost Red

Tussie Mussie
Our last song
A nonsense!

Our nosegay
Perverse!
A posy

What lavender?
Compared to her
Sweet geranium

My stockings
Mocked
Ladders
Leaving you
Only shredded Red
Holding us together
Petals strewn

Life stop
Weaving
My "pink rosebud" longings
Do you decline my leafy angelic ring?
Angels live
In me
Tussie Mussie
Angels!

Pure heavenly cherubim
Leaving snail snow
Showing you
White sheets and violets
Geranium and rosebuds
Stained lives lost ribbons
Red and Red and Red
Forever

During the 1700s people liked to send messages to their friends
by means of small bunches of flowers and herbs called tussie
mussies. This was called 'floriography'. Different flowers and

herbs stood for different feelings. By the nineteenth century, there were even floral dictionaries, and mothers taught their daughters the language of flowers. A tussie mussie became a way to say things that people were too shy to say out loud.

Erotichim v Eroticher

CUMIN
Purée with cumin
My pulses run high
I take your mushroom Wellington
Leeking
Buckwheat
Crepes
You squash my spirit
With those Moorish overtones
Come to my watercress bed
Come
Cumin
Come
Cumin
Feta and fettered
My baby spinach
Your pink ginger
My brazen chicory
See me dressing

JULIE MULLEN

My minty dumplings
Dangle and mess with
Me! Saffron
We artichoke together
We Dijon together
Olive bound
Giving petits pois
Free range to be
Organic
Gnocchi
Gnocchi
Gnocchi
I touch walnuts now
Greek yoghurt spurts
Mosh
Nosh
Wash
Your courgette kofta spits
Deep frying
For the sauce
Very finely chopped

Cumin
Cumin
Cumin
My minty dumplings
Flageolet
Cumin
Cumin
Cumin
My nuts roasted now
Cumin
Cumin
Cumin
Falafel
Cheese
And split pea

JULIE MULLEN

Marrow Me

LASHED WITH RAIN
I grizzled and drizzled to the solitary part
   of my life
My patch
My place
Deep deep down I dug for you
Deep deep down I sung for you
Deep deep down I assumed you would be there
I would take you into my kitchen
I would wash you gently
Stroking your strong hold
Your vitality
But I had to cut you free first
Oh marrow I have dreamt of this day
You of shape
You of story
You of deep penetration
In my soils
In my spoils

Erotic Poetry for Vegans & Vegetarians

You look sad
Freshly bespoke
Near the artichoke
I almost softly spoke
But
Why
You're shuddering
Are you scared
That I may compare you
To other marrows that have come before
I cannot let you mine under yourself
Marrow I say
Marrow you have been chosen
By me
By me
I see you weaken
Your green outer skin
Browns
You look smaller
You look shrivelled
I take soft lighting

Possess a shirt around you
A Vivienne Westwood pure white linen shirt
Soft
I see an awakening
You take your rightful place
Vivienne has woven her magic
She has made you proud to be a marrow
Come hither marrow
I take you to my altar
And I confess to you that from seed
You were always in my sights
I used to watch you from my full window
Green grass blushed at my stare
I would glare at you from seed
You see marrow I knew
That you and I would have destination together
So come marrow come
I open myself to you
I have dressed you with olive oils
I have spent time massaging your tender tender
Are you ready marrow

Erotic Poetry for Vegans & Vegetarians

Ready ripe and mellow
Marrow me
I turn the wedding music up
Marrow me
Gently tell Vivienne to go
Marrow me
And naked now I place you in my soil
In my soul
To grow to grow

JULIE MULLEN

The Landscape Man

HE WAS THERE again
The Landscape Man
He kept me squarely parked

He was my fantasy landscapery
Tersely
And cursory
Scapegoatery
Kind of narked

He was the tenderer
He was the soiler
I was a square peg
A buns-on-boiler

He was a con cedar
An earth feeder
A completer
A roman seater

It was sleeting
So what could he be completing
I rang his bell
Oh what the hell
I wanted to be needed
Especially and
Overly
Ovary
Rarely seeded

I rang the bell
The bell on his door
But no answer
Oh bore
Oh bore

I called his phone
And down the line
I began to moan and sign
I spoke of soil
I spoke of dirt

I told him of my rubber skirt
I told him I was solid oak
That this phone call was no joke
That's when he began to spoke
He spoke
Be spoke
We spoke
Bespoke

It was landscape chat
All measuring and feeling
At last at last he was doing all the revealing

He spoke in lengths
He spoke in dig
He spoke in fractions
He spoke in zig

Can I come in
I waited
Paused

But his contracts didn't contain that licentious
    clause

I told him of my vegetable allotment
A lonely lonely bed
But he just ranted on about his bloody nouveau
    shed

I begged him
I shouted
I opened up my guts
But according to his lawyers
He was keeping those fine nuts

I said I would strip off
Cover myself in chaff "Do it," he said
"Do it" 'cos he needed a good laugh

I stripped off naked
My structure
Gaze askew

JULIE MULLEN

My landscaping darling redeemed my
Portrait, I knew

His face was cold
His hands all moist
Rendering me
Dash pebble then
Dew
Wet wet wet
We went
Wetwet wetwet
Wetwetwet we went wet all through

He loaded
He exploded
We scaped
Draped
And dived

My landscape garden
Was shaped and seeded

All that was needed
Now thrived

My garden was full
My land
My love
Was null was null
Avoiding
My landscape lover
Was like no other
Measured
Never mis-
Leading
Left me
Landscapery
Needing needing
Scapegoatery
Bleeding bleeding

JULIE MULLEN

Angelica & Her Brazilian

Aren't you cold
warm me
Why did you do it
cool me
Didn't it hurt
razor light
Why did you do it
curious night
Can I dress it
alarming
Smother it and press it
charming
I want to feed it
show me
I'll grow some things
bedazzle me
Some herbs some planted
seething me
I thought you'd love it

driving me
I don't mean pot head
slow me
Just something potted
besotted me
I want to herb you
ruin me
I want to spice you up
hot me
I want to dress it nice
sugar me
I think I'll try mint
spear me
I think you'd love clover
Dover me
I want to rub cardamom
over and over me
Will dill do
over and over me
Bay and caraway
over and over

Chamomile and bergamot
rub it rub it extend your plot
I want to borage you
help me help me
Hop and hyssop
recover me reconcile me
Oh sweet cicely
thyme melilot
Hey pesto
A herb pillow
Your tussie mussie
is going to thrill you
I am caraway now
boraged and bay
I cannot farewell
c'est vraie
You mean savoury?

Sexy Pizza

Y OU SEXY SEXY pizza you
   Look at you
All cheesy and full of mouth
Watering
Succulent
Tempting
Cheese
You wheat allergy
You dairy allergy
You sugar allergy
You make me dance for my
Solitary carrot
The pizza must be shoved

JULIE MULLEN

Bent Not Just Crooked

H E WAS BENT not just crooked
I handed him a plain piece of paper
To write his last will and testimony
I was his witness
I'd met him in a tea shop
His cup ran over
Mine — was empty
He was bent not just crooked
But his smile filled my empty cup

And all at once I was bent and not just crooked
No longer alone
I followed him home
Uninvited
I stayed with him all night
We made love to George Formby
We were just "Leaning On A Lamppost"
Him 77 me 19

He died once, twice then came
Back and at breakfast
He wrote his will leaving me
This bent not just crooked stranger's all

I didn't like to ask

Two months later I was
Sent a letter from a firm of solicitors
Enclosed was that 78 record
And a cheque
I smiled
No longer bent yet most deafeningly crooked
I left for the café
For tea for tea

JULIE MULLEN

To Be Vegan

A SOFT LAVENDER
Brushed under the carpet
As I left for work
This morning
I worked in town
I caught the tube
It was crowded
So crowded but
 A man gave me his seat
His hand touched me
As I accepted his seat
He was pressed hard against my leg
He was older
Tanned
Sure
With a slight smile that
Seemed unsure
So I gave my slight unsure smile
Back

He was reading
Soon I was reading into
His mind
Was he
Was he
Was he
Was he
Was he
Around
Available
Free
For me
Was he
Was he
Was he
Was he
Was he
Was he
Or simply wasn't he
So I read but didn't read
And that hard pressing

Helped me
Helped me
Helped me
It plunged me into head silence
I felt something
I hadn't felt in some time
A great big banging loveness
A huge crowded house kind of loveness
He was French
His paper told me that
I was Irish
English
Irish
Oh gibberish really
Now
Then a seat came free next to me
And he took it
It was his honour
It was his time
And I was touching
His hip

He was touching mine
I was hungry suddenly
Really hungry
So hungry
And thirsty
And hot
Terribly hot
I was coming down with something
Something
It was him
I gibbered inside trying so hard to
Remember all my French
Oh god
Oh god
Merde
Then I sensed an aroma
A slight aroma of sandalwood
It was on him
I sensed a smell of leather
A real smell of leather
Coming from him

JULIE MULLEN

I looked down and saw his shoes
They were leather
LEATHER
I couldn't control myself
Any longer
I took his shoes off
Without asking him and I
dragged them to my nose
Oh crumbs but I'm vegan

About the Author

Julie Mullen is a Liverpool Poet. She takes her inspiration from Brian Patten, Roger McGough, Philip Larkin and Sylvia Plath. She worked as an actress for 20 years before discovering the poet within. Julie Mullen now lives in Teddington by the Lock, running The Word Café for poets, musicians and wordsmiths.

www.juliemullen.com